DEDICATED

This Book 'Things of Trading You Should Learn About' is dedicated to the New Traders Who Starts There New Journey In The World Of Trading. In This Book You Will Learn All Of Basic Needs That New Trader Should Know Basics of Trading, Risk Management, Money Management, Trading Psychology Technical Analysis in Very Simple And Easy Words So Lets Begin To Start Your Journey.

Content

Chapter - 1

Basics Of Trading

(Types Of Charts, Trends, Volume, Important Chart Pattern, Candlestick Reversal Patters)

1. Types of Charts

Charts are two-dimensional representation of price over time. There are many types of charts available. But most popular and widely used among them are Line Charts, Bar Charts and the Candlestick Charts. The X axis, i.e. the time axis is crucial. The unit can be month, week, day, hour, 5 min or few seconds. The shorter the time period, more detailed the chart becomes. The beauty of time in technical analysis is that the same concepts apply to charts irrespective of time frame of observation. However, the success rate of individual patterns or indicators-based decisions may vary across time frames. Generally higher the time frame of chart, relatively higher is the probability of any concept in market.

1.1: Line Charts:

In line chart each and every price point is represented as a dot. The X axis represents the time scale and the Y axis represents the price. Each dot or point represents the closing price at the end of a unit of time. These points are then joined to form a line. This is the simplest form of chart. But this is quite good if we want to plot 3-4 similarly priced stocks in a single chart and compare. Moreover, the line chart gives the clearest idea about price direction of a stock.

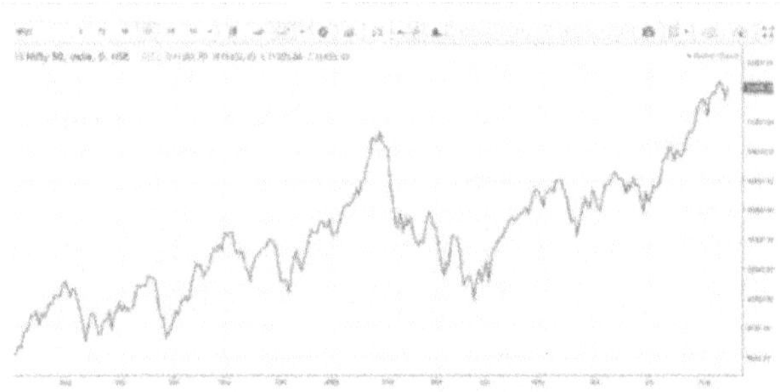

Figure 1.1: Line Chart

1.2: Bar Charts:

A bar chart is comprised of a series of bars. Every bar has four important price points - open close high and low. The bars are represented in green or blue color when close is higher than open and red color when close is lower than open. The bar charts are more detailed than the line chart and are good for demonstrating or spotting the classical price patterns. We will discuss about the classical chart patterns in appropriate time.

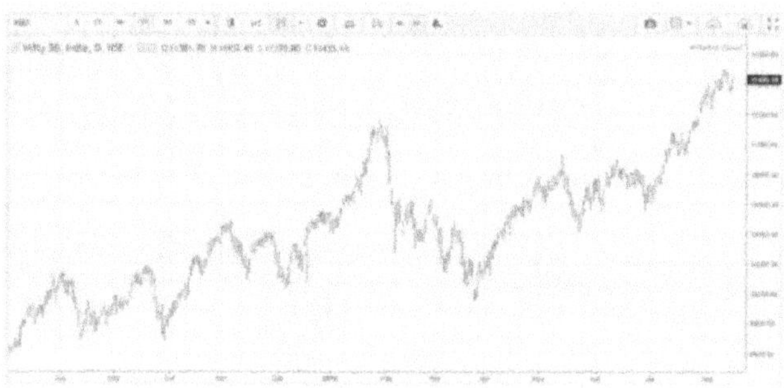

Figure 1.2: Bar Chart

1.3: Candlestick Chart:

The concept of candlestick charts came from Japan. That is why they are often referred to as Japanese candlestick charts. These charts are the most versatile and popular form of chart representation. Price behaviour

r during each time unit is represented in the form of a candle. If the closing price of a stock is higher than open price during a particular time period, then the candle is green, if the close price is below the open price then the candle is red. Each candle has a body and two wicks. The distance between open to close is represented by the body of a candle and the upper and lower wicks represent the highs and lows of a candle.

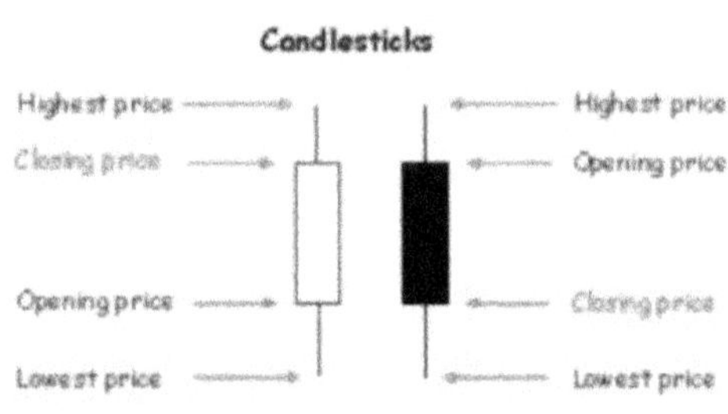

Figure 1. 3(a): Candlestick Chart Diagrammatic Representation

Candlestick chart is special not only because it adds a special visual clarity about the price action, but also because often a single candle stick or two or three consecutive candlesticks together form a pattern that indicate reversal of a prior move or give conviction on continuation of the ongoing move. These are called candlestick patterns. We will discuss about them in due course of time.

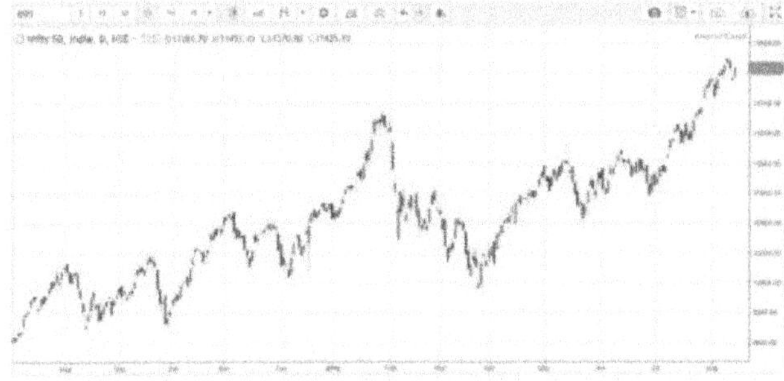

Figure: 1(b): Candlestick Chart Pattern Example

2.Trends

2.1: Market Trend and Range-Bound Consolidation:

Often market movements happen in the form of trends. A price trend is a continuous or a directional price movement in upward or downward direction. We call them up-trend and down - trend respectively. Now if we look at price action in market through charts, we will find that no price movement happens in a straight line. Suppose we are looking at a broader uptrend represented as primary move, we may find intermediate corrections represented as secondary trend and minor counter moves among the secondary moves represented as minor trend. This is how the market behaves generally in both the up and the down trends.

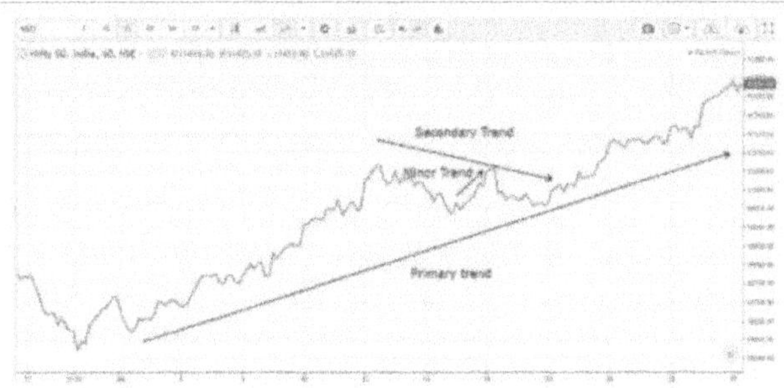

Figure 2.1(a): Market Trends

Often an up-trend is represented in the form of a sequence of higher highs and higher lows. Similarly a downtrend is represented as a sequence of lower lows and lower highs. A trend is said to reverse when the sequence is broken.

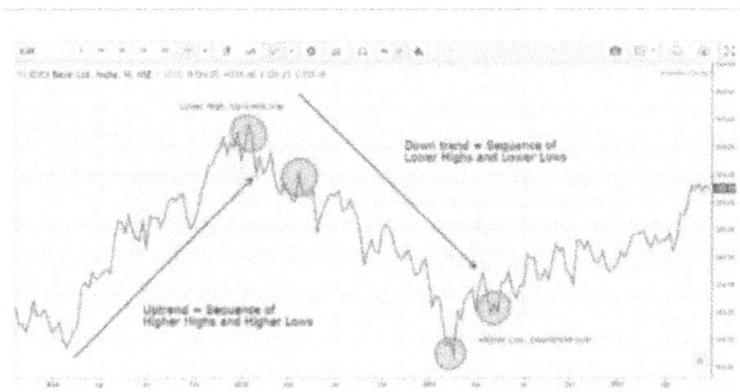

Figure 2.1(b): Trend Reversal

We should remember a simple point that market is not trending all the time. Often the market consolidates within a small range and goes nowhere. Then suddenly it can break on the upside or downside.

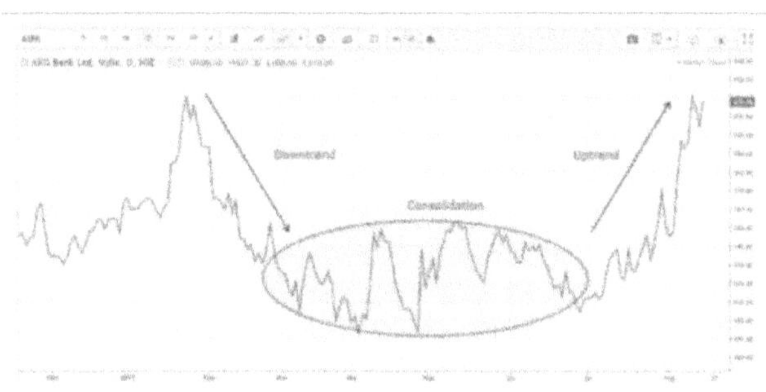

Figure 2.1(c): Market Consolidation

2.2: Trendline & Channels:

Trendline and Channels are one of the most simple and useful tools in the market. During an uptrend, a trendline is formed by joining lowest points of periodic pull-backs, defined as secondary moves in the previous section. The up-trend line has positive slope. To be precise we need two lows to join to form a trendline during an up-move. This line is then extended in the upward direction; the third move towards the trend-line is used to validate the trend line. If the trend line is not broken in the pull back, then it is called trend-line validation. It is often observed that price pulls back towards the trend line and moves higher. In an uptrending market it is often easier to make money if one buys near the trend line and sells higher. The more number of time the trend-line is validated, more important it becomes. An upward trend line is said to be the area of support. The selling pressure meets the buying pressure here and eventually overtime when buying pressure is higher than selling pressure price sees an upward bounce.

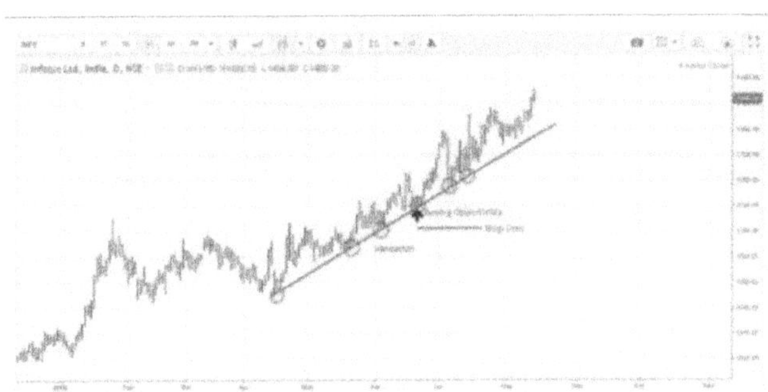

Figure 2.2(a): Uptrend

Now when one buys he or she is looking for the prices to move higher. But this may or may not happen. Hence the investor should maintain a stop loss point below which he or she should cut his position, i.e. book loss. When a trend line is broken, either the market may reverse the trend, continue the uptrend with little less force or just go sideways.

Figure 2.2(b): Uptrend Reversal

Similarly, during a down-trend: a trendline is formed by joining pull-back highs. They slope downwards. Just like an up-trend line a down-trend line is formed by joining two points and then extended in downward direction. Pull backs towards the trend-lines are low risk points for short selling with a stop loss little above the trend line. More number of times the line is validated, more it grows in importance.

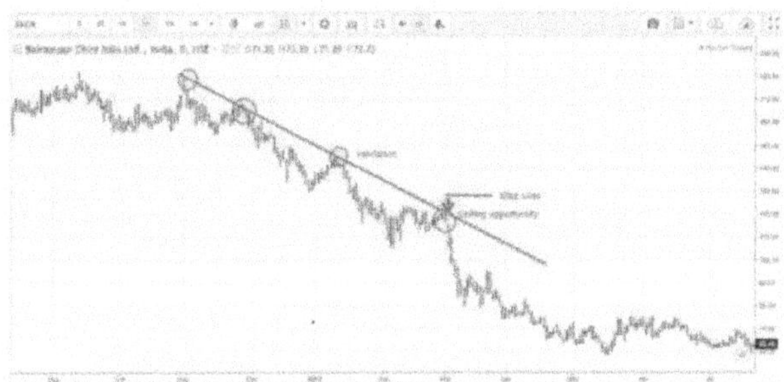

Figure: 2.2(c): Downtrend

Similar to an uptrend-line, when a down trending trend line is broken the trend may continue with less pace, or reverse or may go side-ways. A downward trend line is said to be area of resistance. The selling pressure meets the buying pressure here and eventually overtime when selling pressure is higher than buying pressure price sees a decline.

2.3 Role Reversal:

Once a trendline support or resistance is broken, its role is reversed. If the price falls below a support line, that line will become resistance. If the price rises above a resistance line, it will often become support. As the price moves past a line of support or resistance, it is considered that supply and demand have shifted, causing the breached line to reverse its role. For a true reversal to occur, however, it is important that the prices make a strong move through either the support or resistance line.

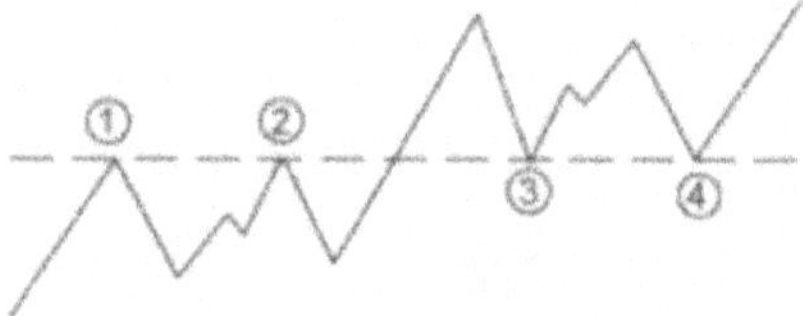

Figure 2.3: Role Reversal

2.4: Channels

The concept of channel is much similar to trend lines. When in an uptrend or in a down trend or in a consolidation, we see rhythmic movement in form of parallelogram, we can draw channels. The channel boundaries are good points for reversal trades with small stop losses.

3. Volume

In this section we introduce the second aspect of charting. This is called volume. Traded volume is the number of quantity of stocks which change hand. The volume is shown as a sub graph in the price-time chart, below the price window. Higher the volume in any particular move, the greater is the conviction in that move to continue greater distance in that direction. However, if volume is on the lower side during a move, the stock is generally bound to lose momentum.

Generally, during range bound phases, the volume is low.

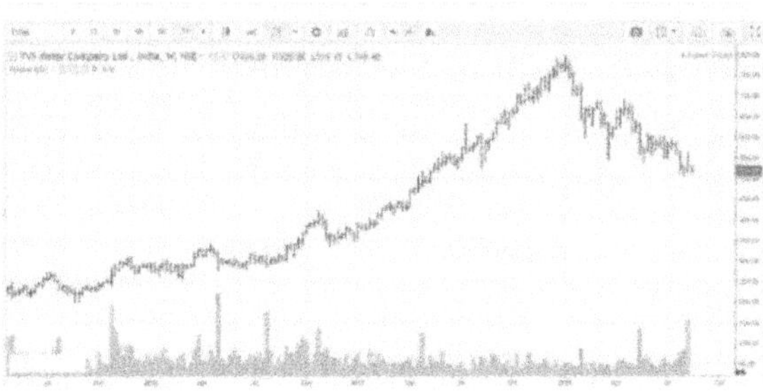

Figure 3: Volume

An important point regarding volume is that traded volume in absolute term has no significance. When we talk about higher or lower volume, it is relative to average volume over certain time periods.

Trend	Volume	Interpretation
Up	High	Uptrend may go greater distance
Up	Low	Lack of conviction/ participation in uptrend. Likely to retrace.
Down	High	Down move may cover greater distance
Down	Low	Less conviction in the down move, may reverse

Apart from traded volume, one important concept regarding volume is delivery %. In the market a person can first buy shares and sell by the end of the day. He or she can do the reverse too. This is called intra-day trading. However, if an investor is having a positive view he may buy the share and carry forward it for a number of days. This is called taking delivery of a share. Hence if there is a price rise of a stock with high % of delivery volume, then this signifies a positive conviction in the stock.

Similarly, if a lot of people are long term negative about a stock, they may sell the stock and give delivery. Markets are driven by buyers and sellers. People who have positive view on a security are called bulls and people who have negative view are called bears. The price of a security in a market is determined by supply-demand dynamics of any stock. If the supply is high and a lot of people look to sell the stock, than there are available buyers, the price is likely to decline. Hence a fall in price with high delivery % is known as negative for a stock.

4. Important Chart Patterns

As we have discussed in the previous section, that market can be either in trending phase or in a range-bound phase. No trend generally lasts forever in the market. After prolonged or medium or shorter duration up and downtrend, the market often reverses and a move starts in the opposite direction of the prior move. Often we find that well defined geometrical patterns are formed in the chart which provides good indication of price reversals. These patterns are called reversal classical chart patterns. When they are formed as a bullish reversal pattern they are said to be part of accumulation. On the other hand if they are formed at the top of a price move just before bearish reversal, then they are part of distribution.

However, a geometrically shaped consolidation does not necessarily mean price reversal. Often price resumes the erstwhile trend post the consolidation move. These are called continuation classical chart pattern. We will discuss about few of the classical chart patterns in the following section.

4.1: Head and Shoulder & Inverse Head & Shoulder:

Head and Shoulder pattern is a bearish reversal pattern. This pattern appears after an uptrend. This pattern is formed with three consecutive tops with middle one being higher than the other two. The middle top is called the head and the two side peaks are called the shoulders. On joining the intermediate troughs, we get the neck-line. On ultimate break below the neckline, usually a short trade is taken with a stop-loss above the top of the nearest shoulder. The target is usually considered as the distance between the neckline and head, projected from the point of break. If the volume in the down leg of the right shoulder is on the higher side and break happens with high volume, the conviction is on the higher side for the reversal.

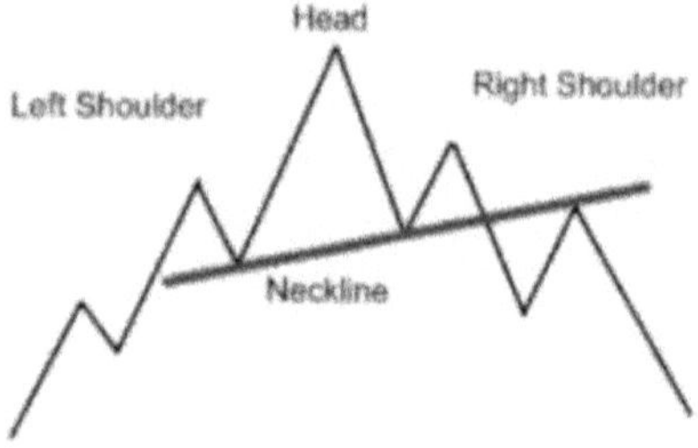

Figure 4.1: Head And Shoulder Pattern

An Inverse Head and Shoulder is just mirror image of the Head and Shoulder pattern. This should appear after a sustained down trend, the rule of stop loss and target are similar. This often acts as a very effective bullish reversal pattern.

4.2 Double Tops and Bottoms:

These chart patterns are well-known patterns that signal a trend reversal - these are considered to be one of the most reliable patterns and are commonly used. These patterns are formed after a sustained trend and signal to chartists that the trend is about to reverse. These patterns are created when price movement tests support or resistance levels twice and is unable to break through. These patterns are often used to signal intermediate and long-term trend reversals.

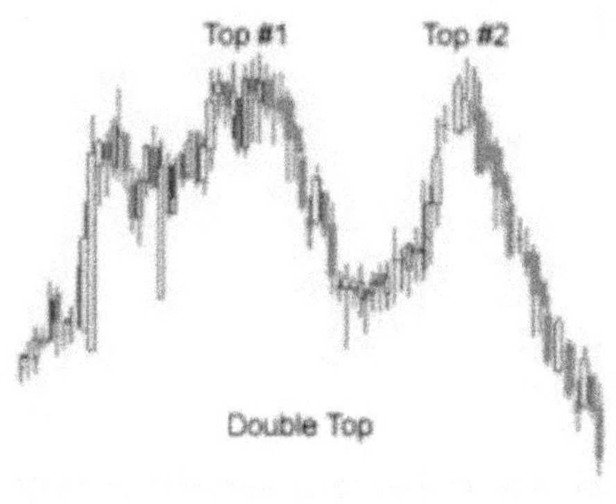

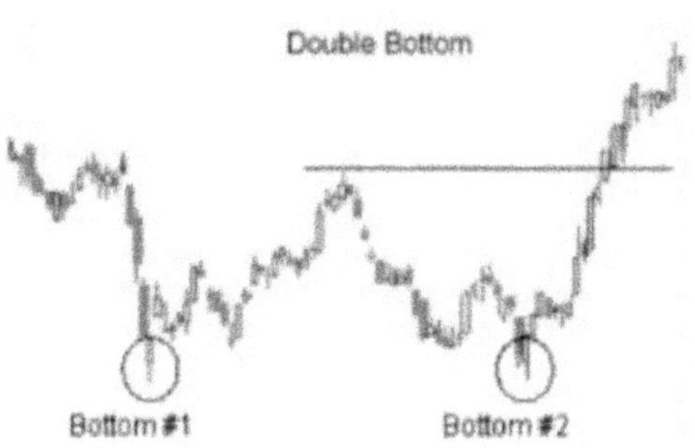

Figure 4.2: Double Tops and Bottoms

4.3: Triple Tops and Bottoms:

These are another set of reversal chart patterns in chart analysis. These are not as prevalent in charts as Head and Shoulders and Double Tops and Bottoms, but they act in a similar fashion. These two chart patterns are formed when the price movement tests a level of support or resistance three times and is unable to break through. They signal a reversal of the prior trend. A trade entry is initiated at the break of a neckline with a small stop-loss and the target is measured as the distance between peaks/troughs and the neckline.

Figure 4.3: Triple Tops and Triple Bottoms

4.4 Triangles:

Triangles are one of the most well-known chart patterns used in technical analysis. The three most common types of triangles, which vary in construction and implications, are Symmetrical Triangle, Ascending Triangle and Descending Triangle. These chart patterns are considered to last anywhere from a couple of weeks (ideally more than 12 weeks) to several months. These are areas of consolidations after a trending move and are generally continuation patterns, i.e. the erstwhile trends resumes after the breakout. However, in certain cases they act as reversal patterns. They can appear both in up-trend and down-trend.

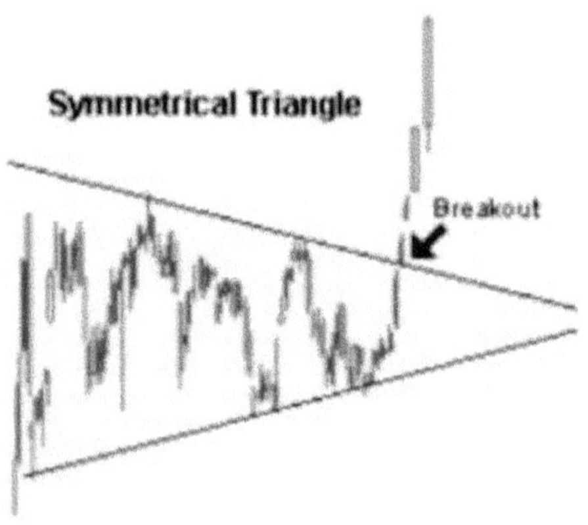

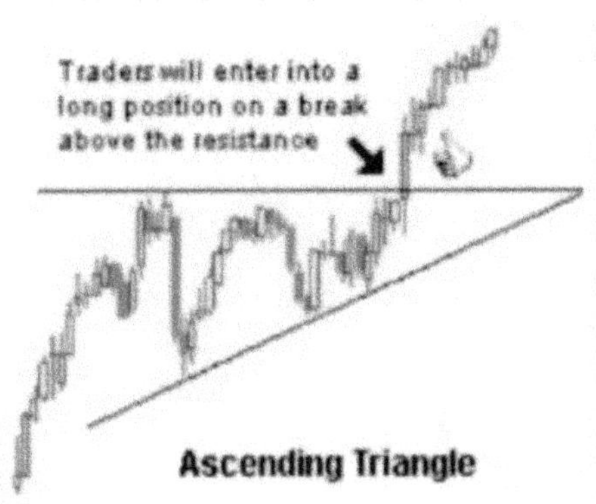

Ascending Triangle

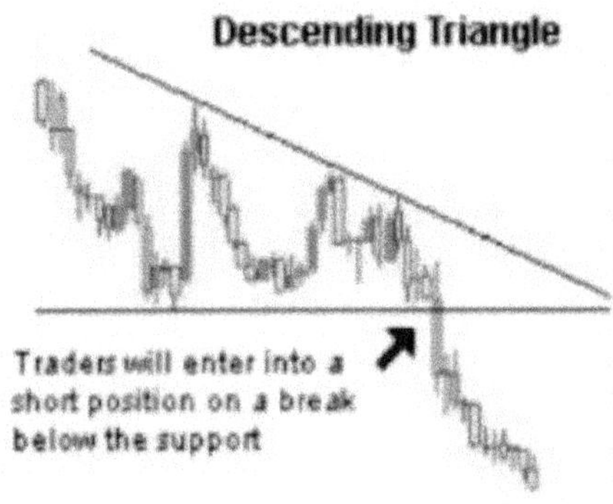

Figure 4.4: Three Kinds of Triangle Patterns

4.5: Flag and Pennant:

These two short-term chart patterns are continuation patterns that are formed when there is a sharp price movement followed by a generally sideways price movement. The patterns are generally thought to last from one to three weeks (Can last from 1 to 12 week but ideally they should last between 1 and 4 weeks). They can appear both in up-trend and down-trend.

Figure 4.5: Flags and Pennants

4.6 Wedge:

The Wedge chart pattern can be either a continuation or reversal pattern. It is similar to a Symmetrical Triangle except that the Wedge Pattern slants in an upward or downward direction, while the symmetrical triangle generally shows a sideways movement. The other difference is that Wedges tend to form over longer periods, usually between three and six months. The fact that Wedges are classified as both continuation and reversal patterns, can make reading signals confusing. However, at the most basic level, a falling wedge in an uptrend is bullish and a rising wedge in a downtrend is considered bearish.

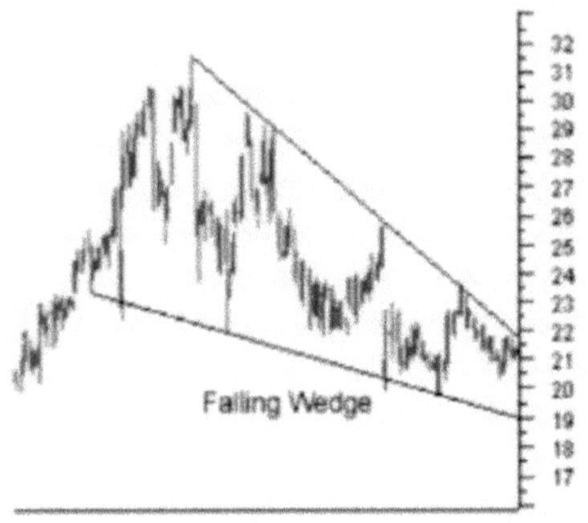

Figure 4.6: Wedges

5 Candlestick Reversal Patters

When we had discussed about the candlestick charts, we had said that they have an edge over many other types of charts representation due to recognizable chart patterns which are easy to define and which work beautifully in the market.

In this section we will discuss about few chart popular candlestick patterns. Candlestick patterns provide entry and stop-loss criteria, but there are no target setup as available in classical chart patterns.

5.1: Hammer:

Hammer is a single candlestick bullish reversal pattern. This occurs after a prolonged down trend. Ideally there should be a gap down opening and bears should be able to push the price lower as a continuation of a down move. At this point, bulls should overpower bears and push price higher and make close near to the opening price. The candle formed in this process should be having a small body, a big lower shadow and a negligibly small upper shadow. Ideally the lower shadow should be at least twice the length of the body. The color of the body can be either green or red, but if the body color is green, then the hammer is considered a little more bullish, as the bulls were strong enough to close the price higher than the open price. The next day or in next two three days, ideally there should be a gap up opening or price should move above the high of the hammer candle. This is called confirmation or validation of the pattern. A hammer like candle, without validation has no real significance. If price moves above the high of the hammer a buy trade can be taken with a stop loss below the low of the candle.

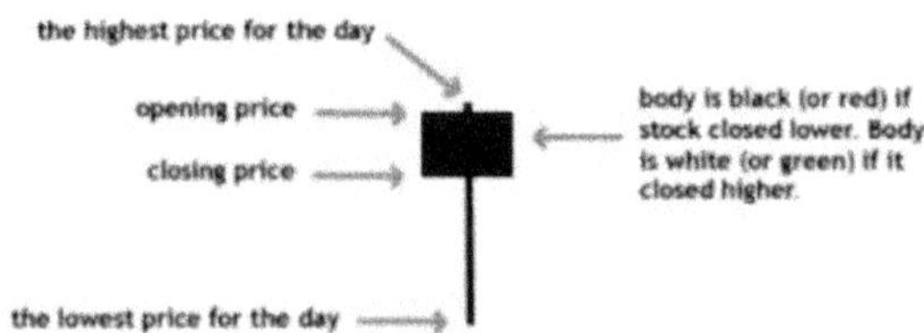

Figure 5.1(a): Hammer

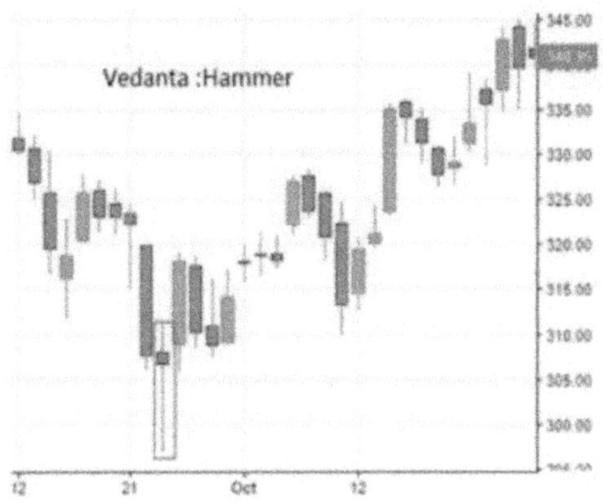

Figure 5.1(b): Hammer Example

5.2: Shooting Star:

A shooting star is just like a mirror image of a hammer candle. First there should be a sustained up trend and then there has to be a gap up opening. The bulls should push price higher in the initial part of the day. Then, later in the day bears should take in the control of the stock and push prices down. Eventually the closing price should be very close to the opening price, resulting in a candle with a small green or red body, a big upper shadow and a small or negligible lower shadow. The upper shadow of the candle should be at least twice the length of

32

the body. Now a confirmation of the shooting star pattern comes if price moves below the low of the candle within next 2-3 candles. On confirmation, a short trade should be taken with stop loss above the high of the high of the candle. A shooting star pattern with a red body is considered slightly more bearish than one with a green body. It is often observed that shooting star candlestick pattern acts as bearish reversal pattern and triggers a down move after an uptrend.

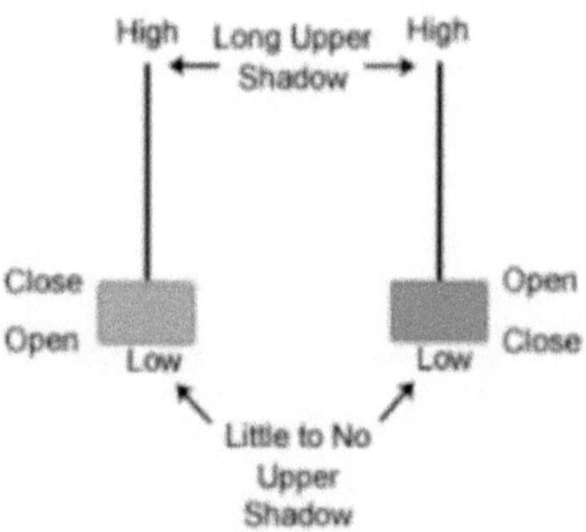

Figure 5.2(a): Shooting Star

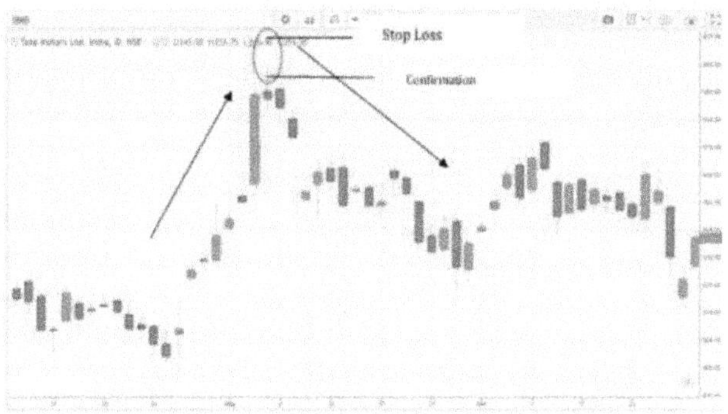

Figure 5.2(b) Shooting Star Example:

5.3: Inverted-Hammer:

An inverted hammer is a single candlestick bullish reversal pattern. The pattern appears after a sustained down-trend. At the beginning of the day there should be a gap-down opening. However, bulls should push the price higher during the course of the day. Eventually the bears should push the price lower during the course of the day and close near the open price. The resulting candle should have a small body, red or green, the upper wick should be at least twice the body of the candle and the lower shadow should be quite small or negligible in size. If the body is green it is relatively bullish than if it is red. This looks like an inverted hammer as the name suggests. The philosophy is that bears were not able to push the price below the opening price during the course of the day. This pattern, however, is considered to be little less bullish than the hammer itself, because in hammer bulls are able to force a higher close by the end of the day. The confirmation of the pattern comes once the price moves above the high of the candle. On confirmation a buy trade can be initiated with a stop loss below the low of the candle. Inverted hammer occurs little less frequently in market as compared to hammer pattern.

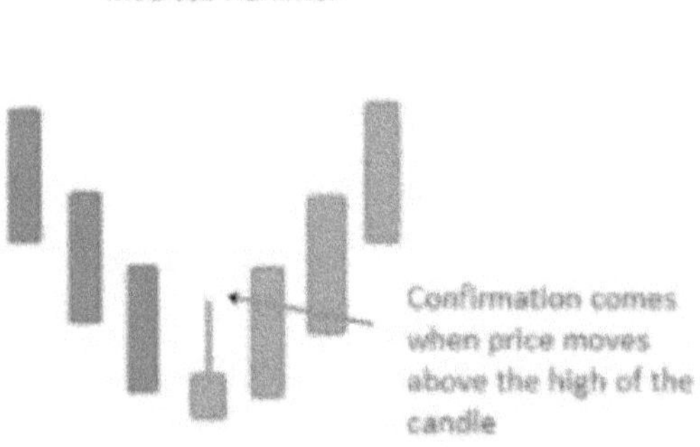

Figure 5.3: Inverted Hammer

5.4: Hanging Man:

Hanging Man is a single candlestick bearish reversal pattern. This appears after a sustained up-move. The candle looks like a hammer; only difference is that it appears at the end of an up-trend. The candle should have a small body at the top (red/green) and a lower shadow at least twice the length of the body. There should be very small or no upper shadow. A red colored body of hanging man pattern is more bearish than a hanging man pattern with green body. The confirmation of the pattern happens when price moves below the low of the candle. On confirmation a trader may take short trade with stop-loss above the high of the candle. The hanging man pattern is bearish counterpart of Bullish inverted hammer. However this appears much less frequently than shooting star which is another bearish reversal pattern.

Figure 5.4: Hanging Man Pattern

5.5: Bullish Engulfing Pattern:

Bullish candlestick pattern is a two-candlestick bullish reversal pattern. First there should be a downtrend. Then we should have a red candle followed by a green candle. The body of the green candle should engulf the body of the first red candle. The idea is in the second candle that constitutes the pattern, the day started below the previous day's close on a bearish note. However, as the day progresses, the bulls take-over the charge and eventually succeed to close above previous day's high. In such a scenario, if the highest point of these two candlesticks is breached on the upside within next 2-3 candles, the bearish engulfing pattern is said to be confirmed. A buy trade can be initiated upon confirmation with stop-loss below the low of the two candlestick patterns.

Figure 5.5: Bullish Engulfing Pattern

5.6: Bearish Engulfing Pattern:

Bearish Engulfing pattern is just mirror image of bullish engulfing pattern with bearish implication. First, we should be having an up-trend. Then we should have a green candle as continuation. The next day should see a gap up above the close of previous day. The 2nd day candle should eventually close red with its body totally engulfing the body of the first candle. The confirmation comes when within next 2-3 candles the price moves below the low of the two candles forming the Bearish Engulfing pattern. On confirmation a trader may take a short trade with stop loss above the top of the two candlestick patterns. Larger the 2nd candle, more bearish is the pattern.

Figure 5.6: Bearish Engulfing Pattern

5.7: Piercing Pattern:

The piercing pattern is just similar to the bullish engulfing pattern; only thing is that the 2nd candle in the two candlestick pattern does not close engulfing the body of the first candle. Instead it closes crossing the halfway mark of the body of the first candle. A confirmation comes when price crosses the high of the two candlestick patterns within next 2-3 candles. On confirmation one may take a buy trade with stop loss below the low of the candle.

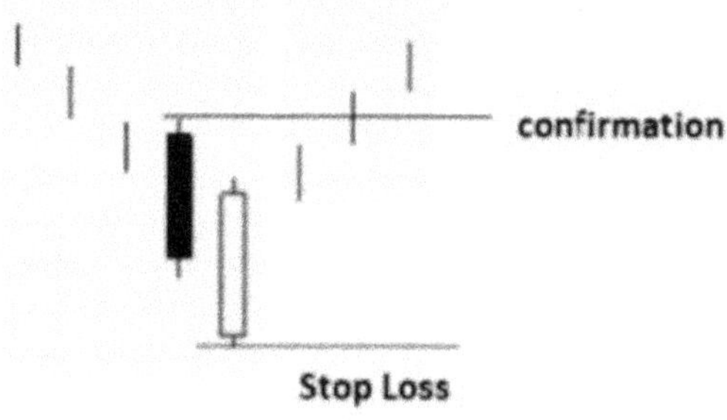

Figure 5.7: Piercing Pattern

5.8: Dark Cloud Cover:

The Dark cloud cover is a two candlestick bearish reversal pattern and much similar to the bearish engulfing pattern. In this pattern, the second candle, unlike the bearish engulfing pattern falls short of engulfing the first candle, instead it crosses 50% the body of the first candle. The confirmation comes when a candle breaches the bottom of the pattern. On confirmation a short trade can be taken with stop loss above the high of the candle.

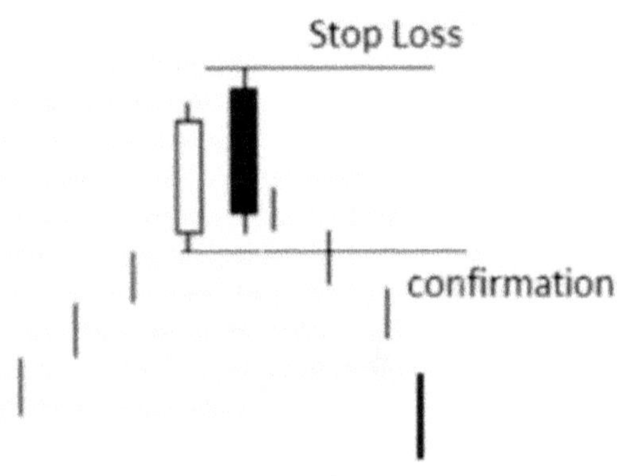

Figure 5.8: Dark Cloud Cover

5.9: Doji:

The Doji is a single candlestick pattern. The Doji assumes significance, when it appears after a trending move, be it up or down. The Doji symbolizes indecision and after a Doji the incumbent trend can reverse, go sideways or continue uptrend. However, appearance of a Doji is a signal of caution that the probability is 125 that the erstwhile trend may be coming to an end. Doji is a candle which has open and close almost at similar level. There can be upper shadows and lower shadows of various proportions.

Figure 5.9: Doji

6. Indicators

Indicators are tools to aid decision making in the market. There are various types of indicators which measures or indicate the trend, the momentum, the volatility and various other aspects in the market. There are thousands of indicators which are derived out of the price and volume data over time. Here we introduce you with four very useful indicators.

6.1: Simple Moving Average:

Simple Moving Average or SMA is a moving average which is calculated by adding the closing price of security prices for the last n-periods and dividing it by the total number of time periods.

For example, suppose we want to calculate the 9 periods SMA of a security price.

First, we will add the last 9 Days Closing Price of the security and then it will be divided by the 9 periods.

Calculation for 9 periods SMA:

$$(P9+P8+P7+P6.... +P1)/9$$

Where,

P=Price

P9= Closing Price 9 days ago

SMA is a Technical indicator which is represented by a line and it is directly plotted on the security price. As per the choice of the trader, the periods can be changed in the SMA indicator.

For shorter-term SMA, we can use 5,8,13 etc. For Medium term 20, 34, 50 and for longer term 100,200 can

be used.

If a medium term moving average is having a positive slope, the trend is considered to be positive in medium term and vice versa.

Price breaching a particular moving average from down to up is considered a bullish sign. Similarly, price breaching a particular moving average from upside and closing below is considered bearish.

If we find a shorter term moving average crossing a medium term moving average from below, often this is called bullish crossover. On the other hand if a shorter term moving average crosses a medium term moving average from upside to below that is called a bearish crossover and often considered a signal of bearishness.

Figure 6.1: Simple Moving Average

6.2: RSI:

Relative Strength Index (RSI) is a momentum oscillator, developed by J. Welles Wilder, which measures the speed and velocity of price movement of trading instruments (stocks, commodity futures, bonds, forex etc.) over a specified period of time.

The objective of RSi indicator is to measure the change in price momentum. It is a leading indicator and is widely used by Technical Analysts over the globe. RŠI can be used to spot a general trend. It is considered overbought when it goes above 70 and oversold when it goes below 30. 30-70 region of RSI is considered to

be normal zone.

6.2.1: Calculation:

The formula for calculating Relative Strength Index is as follows

RSI = 100 - 100 / (1 + RS) RS = Average Gain over specified period/ Average loss over the same period

The default setting for Relative Strength Index is 14, but you may change this value to decrease or increase

sensitivity based on your requirement.

6.2.2: Usage:

There are many kinds of usage of RSI. However most popularly, if we find that, RSI breaching the 70 level and at the same time we spot a bearish reversal pattern, then there is opportunity to take short trade with stop loss. Similarly if RSI breaches 30 from below and we observe a bullish reversal pattern, there is opportunity to take long trade with stop loss.

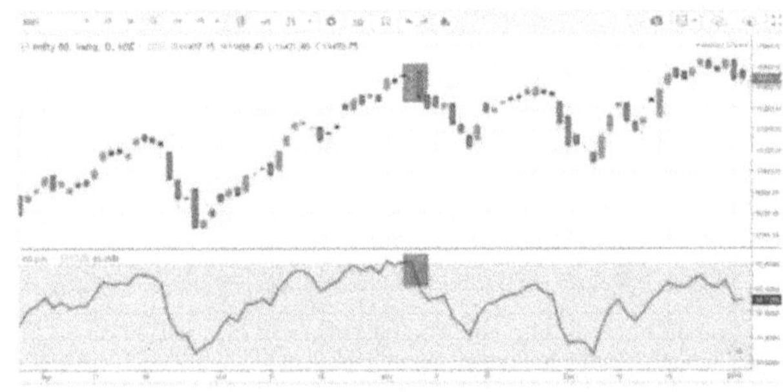

Figure 6.2: RSI

6.3: ADX:

In 1987]. Welles Wilder developed the Average Directional Index (ADX) as an indicator of trend strength.

ADX quantifies the velocity of price regardless of its north/south/eastward movement. Hence, two other lines i.e. Positive Directional Indicator (+DI) and Negative Directional Indicator (-DI) are used on the charting system which act as complements to ADX.

When ADX is above 20 or 25, generally Market is considered to be in a trending phase. The trend can be up or down.

On the other hand, +DI crosses - Di line from below, the market generally moves up and when the -Di line crosses the + Di line from below, market generally moves in the downward direction.

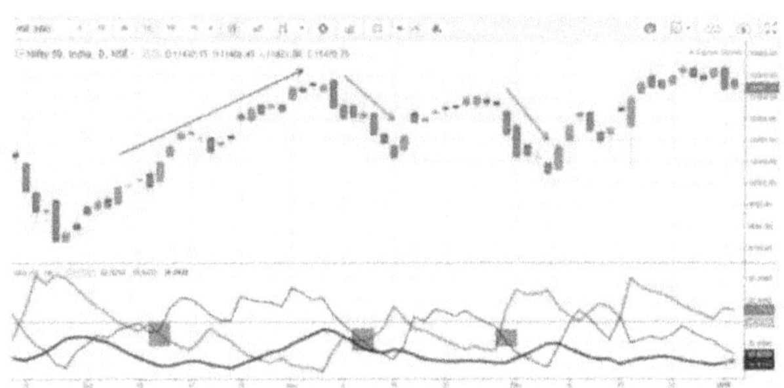

Figure 6.3: ADX

Chapter - 2

Supply And Demand Zone

For a simple real world example think of the price of petrol / gas. When there is a lot

of gas around and there is a large amount of supply, then the price will fall and be

cheaper.

However, on the flip side, if the demand increases and there is less supply

available, then people will start to pay higher prices.

Supply and demand can be seen on everything from house prices through to the amount you pay for your food.

1. What is Supply and Demand in Trading?

Supply and demand works the same way in Forex trading. so lets understand With Example of Forex Trading. If there is a large amount of demand for a certain currency, then it will rise. If however, the demand falls away and there becomes an imbalance where there is too much supply, then just like in the real world the price will start to fall.

The easiest way to think about this is what happens when price starts rising rapidly in a rising market. As price begins to surge higher more and more traders are trying

to enter (an increase in demand). Because there is not enough supply to keep up with this rising demand the price rises higher.

There are many ways to spot supply and demand levels on your Forex charts. Common ways are trendlines, support and resistance and even using dynamic support and resistance with moving averages.

However, the easiest ways for you to spot supply and demand levels on your charts is with major support and resistance levels. These levels where price continually bounces from show a consistent level where price is finding an oversupply and a level where demand grows.

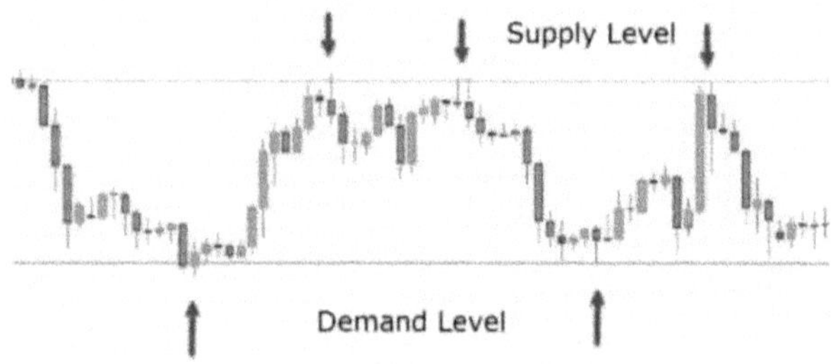

Figure 1

2. How to identify Supply and Demand in the Any Market?

Price is in a constant tug of war between the buyers and sellers. This tug of war is to figure out the supply and demand levels and ultimately who is in control of the next move.

As the example chart shows below, as price moves lower there is an oversupply and a lack of demand. This sends prices lower. Price moves into a demand level (support) where the market dynamics shift. At this level that amount of demand picks up and because demand is now higher, the supply starts to get lower. This sends prices back higher.

As price moves back higher traders start to cash out of their profitable trades. Because traders are leaving their positions and selling out, all of a sudden there is more supply around. What happens when there is more supply and not as much demand? Price starts to fall back lower again.

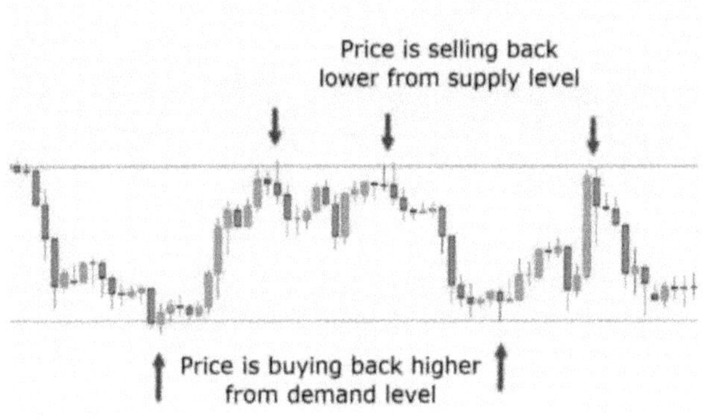

Figure 2

3. Supply Demand Price Action Trading

Whilst there are many complicated ways you can start to use supply and demand levels in your trading, the easiest and often the best is with a clean price action chart.

What does a clean price action chart mean? No indicators or any other distractions. Just raw price action.

See the example chart below. First you notice that price is in a trend higher. You then want to find long trades inline with the current trend. As this example chart shows, you get two potential trading signals to make a long entry.

Price first pulls back into a clear demand (support) area where you could enter long. Price then makes a second pullback into the same demand zone before making another large move higher.

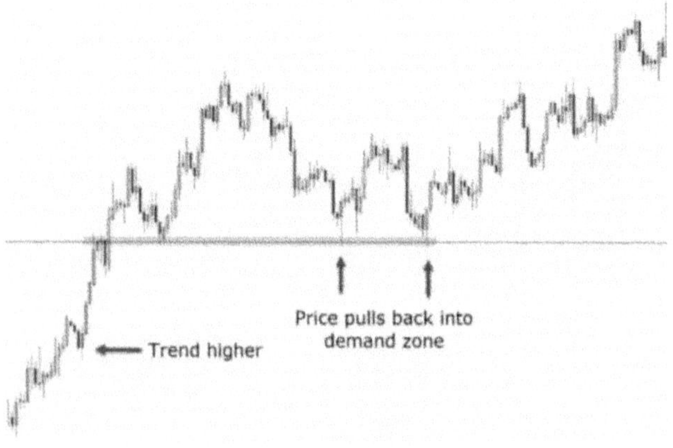

4. Finding Supply and Demand Trading Signals

Once you have learned how to spot obvious supply and demand zones on your charts, you can then start using them to find both high probability trades and also manage your trades.

You can use these levels to make very high reward trades and also to set your stop loss and profit targets. You can also use these same levels on all time frames.

5. Simple Supply and Demand Trading Strategies

The next two examples of supply and demand trades are setups you will see and be able to use in your trading over and over again. They form on all time frames and repeat themselves time and again.

In the first example you identify a clear demand level. Price has clearly found demand at this level multiple times. If you are very aggressive you could just enter a long trade right from this level.

If you are more conservative you could look to increase the odds of your trade by using a bullish Japanese candlestick to confirm your trade. In this example price forms a bullish engulfing bar at the demand level to confirm a long trade higher.

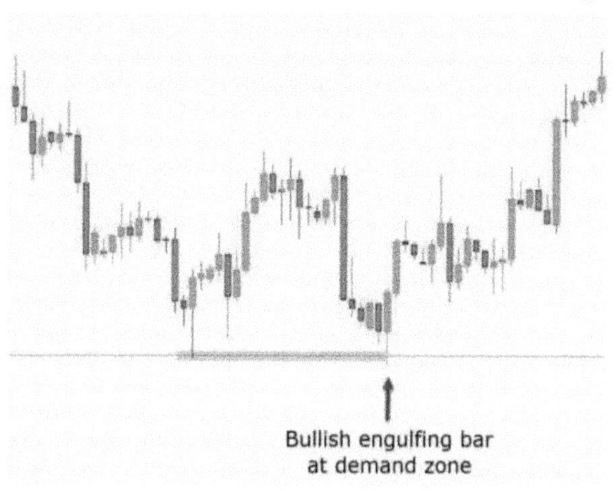

Figure 5.1

In the second example you notice that price is starting to make a move and trend lower. You also notice price break through a clear support level. When price moves back into this supply level you could start looking for short trades. Short trades here would be at an obvious supply level and inline with the trend lower. Just like the first example you could also use a candlestick pattern to confirm the bearish move lower. In this example price forms a shooting star pattern to signal a move back lower.

Figure 5.2

6. Lastly

Being able to accurately identify and use supply
and demand levels can take some time and
practice.

It is not as easy as downloading and using an
indicator that tells you what to do and what
direction to trade.

However, there are many benefits to supply and demand trading once you have mastered it. You can use it to find trades on all time frames and it will also help you with your stops and profit targets.

Make sure you test out any new strategies on free demo charts before you ever risk any real money so you know that they work for you and you are completely comfortable with them.

Chapter - 3
Money Management

It does not matter how great your strategy is; if you don't have good trading money management skills, you will lose money,

A good money management strategy will allow you to ride out the losses and capitalize on the large winners to make you profitable.

In this post, we go through exactly what money management in your trading is and how to use some core strategies.

Money Management Strategies

Some straightforward and easy-to-follow money management rules can immediately help your trading.

Only Risk Money You Can Afford to Lose

This should go without saying, but it is not always followed.

Trading can be risky and you should only risk money that you can afford to lose.

If you have to use money that you should be using for daily expenses, or you are using a loan or credit card, you will be at risk of losing money you cannot afford to.

The other side of this is that if you are using money to trade with that you really need, you will be trading with 'scared' money. So when using money that you cannot afford to lose, you will make poor trading decisions and constantly worry about losing.

Use a Stop Loss

This is another simple strategy that should always be followed but is not.

Using a smart stop loss can ensure you have small losses and then capitalize on your winners.

The best stop loss placements will be at levels where the trade has failed, and instead of having a large loss, you cut it quickly.

Figure 1

2. Calculate Your Risk for Each Trade

If you correctly calculate your risk on each trade, then you can make sure you are risking the right amounts.

For example, some traders will not calculate how much they should be trading each trade and will use the same amount. If you do this, you could risk wildly different amounts on different pairs and stop-loss levels.

The best way to control your risk is to have set rules. For example, you will only risk 2% (3% - 4% for members having capital size 25,000 To 1,00,000) of your account each trade. Before each trade, you use a position size calculator to work out how much you should be trading, so you never risk too much.

3. Money Management Strategies for Serious Traders

If you are a serious trader, you will use other more advanced strategies to ensure your losses stay small and your winners put you in profit.

Have a Minimum Risk-Reward Ratio

A minimum risk-reward ratio for each trade you take will ensure you can come out profitable even after taking on losses.

In the example below, we are taking a long breakout trade. If the price moves lower into our stop loss level, we will automatically stop out of the trade.

However, in this example, the price moves higher and we could take profit at four times that amount we risked or 1:4 risk-reward. This means that if we were risking *2%* on the trade, we would have profited 8%.

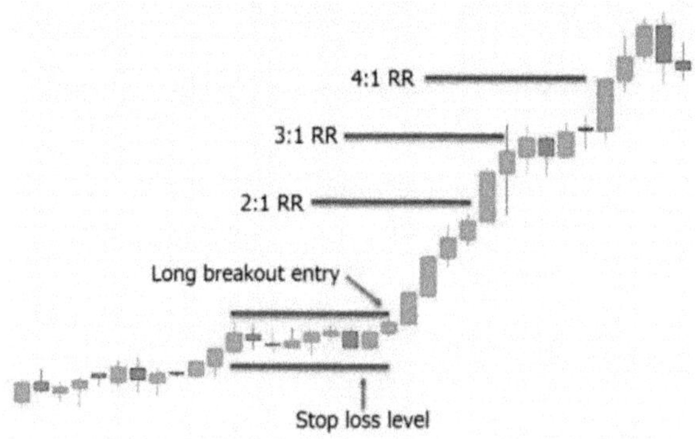

Figure 2

4. Use Leverage Wisely

Leverage is a double-edged sword. You can use it t boost your winners into much larger winners, but it can quickly crush your account if not used correctly.

The best way to make sure you are not using too much leverage is to calculate what trade size you should be using before each trade.

Like in the example above, if we are going to risk 2% each trade, we would use a <u>position size calculator</u> before opening a new trade.

As our account gets bigger or smaller, we would continue risking 2% and making sure we are not using too much leverage.

5. Money Management Plan

The best way to ensure you are staying on track with your money management strategies is to create a clear rule set and money management plan.

This money management plan should include;

#1: Calculate Your Acceptable Risk Per Trade

There are two common methods to working out how much you want to risk per trade.

The first is the fixed percentage method. With this method, you decide how many percent of your account you want to risk per trade, for example, 2%, and you continue to risk 2% as your account gets bigger or smaller.

The second method is the fixed money method. With this method, instead of using a percentage of your account, you risk the same amount of money on each trade. For example, you might have a $5,000 account and choose to risk $250 on each trade.

#2: Calculate What Your Maximum Account Drawdown is

Understanding and using a smart <u>drawdown</u> level can help stop you from blowing your account or putting huge chunks in it.

You may decide that if you lose 25% of your account, it is time to take a break and work out what is going wrong. You may decide to move back to a demo account to find what errors you are making before moving back to your live account.

Having a drawdown level set where you will have a break can help you have a clear rule set around when it's time to pause risking real money.

#3: Create a Ruleset for How You Take Profit and Use Your Stop Loss

Many traders have clear rules around what trades they will take, but they don't have clear stop loss and take profit rules.

You only win or lose money when you close your trade, so it is crucial you have a clear rule set that outlines how you take profit or cut your losses short.

This ruleset can help you minimize your losses and take advantage of the larger winners.

#4: Create a Money Management Plan and Follow it

The best trading plan will be written down with a clear rule set that is easy for you to follow.

Your money management plan should include rules around;

1. How much leverage you use.
2. How much you risk in percentage or money terms.
3. What your acceptable account drawdown is.
4. What minimum risk-reward you will try to achieve for each trade.
5. How you will use correlation.
6. How you will set your take profit and stop-loss levels.

Chapter – 4

Technical Analysis

Technical analysis is the prediction of price movement on a chart of a particular currency pair and other markets. It evaluates securities and identifies trading opportunities by gathering information by analyzing statistics from trading activity.

Using the information you gather from your technical analysis, you can find and make high probability trades.

This post goes through exactly what technical analysis is and how you can use it in your own trading to start making trades with different strategies.

1. What is Technical Analysis?

Technical analysis trading focuses on charts and graphs and how the different price movements on these charts play out.

Understanding these charts and graphs will help you evaluate securities (or Forex pairs and other markets) and forecast the future by analyzing statistics and the price action.

Technical analysis traders have a core assumption that the price is always correct. Technical analysis traders are not looking at what could happen with the fundamentals because they believe that all known possible fundamental information is already factored into the current price.

Figure 1

MACD

The MACD is another hugely popular indicator used in many different markets by technical analysis traders.

The MACD is used to find new trends or momentum.

The MACD has three main part that is;

• MACD line: is created by taking a longer-term EMA and subtracting it from a shorter-term EMA

• Signal line: used to generate buy and sell signals.

Histogram: measures the distance between MACD and its signal line.

Technical analysis, on the other hand, is not taking into account these pieces of information. A trader using technical analysis will be using their charts and other statistics to make their trades. The information the technical analysis trader takes into account includes price trends, indicator information, and a range of different chart patterns that could help them find where the price is moving next.

2. Getting Started in Technical Analysis

Getting started with technical analysis trading is very easy.

Whilst it is easy, that does not mean there is not a lot to learn and that you will be constantly be testing and perfecting new methods.

The best way to get started is to get a free set of demo trading charts and beginning to practice some simple technical analysis strategies in a no-risk environment.

With a demo account, you can practice your technical analysis without risking any real money and start to use more advanced strategies like the ones we go through below.

3. Mastering Technical Analysis

There is a lot to master when it comes to becoming a technical analysis trader. You can choose to use just raw price action, a combination of price action andindicators, or a range of different strategies altogether.

No matter what strategy you decide to use, you will need to keep some things in mind that include;

• You will need to have a solid risk to reward ratio trading strategy.

• You will need a strategy that can handle losses and make money overall.

• You will need a strict rule set that is easy to follow and replicate.

*Y*ou will need to track your trading and constantly improve as the markets change.

One of the hardest parts of trading technical analysis is that it can be hard to develop a clear rule set for making your trades. This is crucial, so you begin to create consistent and repeatable results in your trading.

One way you can do this is with a clear trading plan.

Another thing to keep in mind with technical analysis is that you will not win all of your trades. The goal is to have a system that can handle losses, but it consistently makes you money at the end of the month.

4. The Best Technical Analysis Indicators

4.1 Moving Averages

Moving averages are one of the most popular indicators in the world for technical analysis. You can use moving averages for smoothing out the overall price action to find clear trends and dynamic support and resistance.

When you combine <u>mul</u>tiple moving averages on your chart, you can also find high-quality trade signals.

At its simplest, the moving average shows you the overall price for a certain period of time. For example, if using 14-period moving averages, then you will see the average price for the last 14 periods plotted as a line on your chart. This can show you the overall direction price has been moving in on that time frame.

The two most common moving averages are the SMA: simple moving average and the EMA: exponential moving average.

Figure 4.1

4.2 MACD

The MACD is another hugely popular indicator used in many different markets by technical analysis traders.

The MACD is used to find new trends or momentum.

The MACD has three main part that is;

• MACD line: is created by taking a longer-term EMA and subtracting it from a shorter-term EMA

• Signal line: used to generate buy and sell signals.

Histogram: measures the distance between MACD and its signal line.

Figure 4.2

4.3 Fibonacci Tool

The Fibonacci tool is an indicator you can use to both make and manage your trades.

Fibonacci is formed with a set of key ratio numbers that include 23.6%, 38.2%, 50%, 61.8%, and 100%.

These key levels will often work as important support or resistance levels as they are heavily watched and trades by many participants in the market.

In the example below price is in a trend lower. After making a retracement back higher, we can see the price move into the 61.8% Fibonacci level, where it finds resistance and sells back lower with the trend.

Figure 4.3

5. Advanced Technical Analysis

Some of the most advanced technical analysis strategies involve combining different methods and strategies. These include combining multiple indicators or combining indicators with price action strategies.

In the example below, we are combining multiple moving averages with price action signals.

As the chart example shows, we have a moving average crossover that shows us that there is a trend lower. Price then forms a <u>bea</u>rish engulfing <u>bar</u> that is a bearish price action signal and is a signal to make short trades with the trend lower. This is just one example of how you can combine strategies for more advanced technical analysis.

Figure 5

Chapter - 5

Trading Psychology

The greatest enemy of the trader is fear. He who is afraid loses! As a trader you must have gone through emotions such as fear, greed, regret, hope, overconfidence, doubt, nervousness etc. While every trader goes through this emotional rollercoaster, a successful trader knows that it's never a good idea to let your emotions influence your investment decisions. Not letting your emotions affect your trading decisions is the real meaning of trading psychology! In this article, we will educate you on the meaning of trading psychology. We will also reveal trading tips and tricks to mentally prepare you to trade with confidence!

So, let's begin!

1. What is Trading Psychology?

Trading psychology or investor psychology refers to the trader's emotional and mental state which dictates their trading actions. Some of these emotions like hope, confidence are helpful and should be embraced. But emotions like fear and greed must be contained. Another emotion that is very common in financial markets is the fear of missing out or FOMO. It is essential to understand and develop a sharp mindset along with knowledge and experience to become a successful trader. Let us take a look at the various psychological factors that affect a trader's mindset and some pro-tips to deal with them.

1.1 Fear

Fear is a natural reaction that we sense when something is at risk. While trading, risks could occur in many forms - Some bad news about the stocks or the market. Placing a trade and realising it's not going the way you had hoped. Fear of loss of capital Traders generally overreact and tend to liquidate their holdings because of fear. A strong trading psychology is when traders do not let fear dictate their buy/sell strategy.

1.1.1 What should you do?

Every trader must first understand what they are afraid of and why? Reflect on these issues ahead of time so you can quickly identify the problem and find a solution. Your focus should be to not let the fear of loss refrain you from making profit.

1.2 Greed

Greed enters when you desire excess profits. Rome was not built in a day and neither will your stock market fortune. If you find yourself on a winning streak, then book your profits and move on. Majority of the time, your greed will turn a winning streak into a disaster!

1.2.1 What should you do?

To combat greed, you should have a predefined profit booking level. Even before you enter a trade, define your stop-loss and book-profit levels to avoid being swayed by greed. A sound trading psychology is when you are content with your profits and do not chase irrational profits.

1.3 Regret

Regret in trading comes in two ways. A trader could regret placing a trade that didn't work or Regret not placing a trade that could have worked. A trading psychology based on regret can be dangerous for a trader as it may result in placing wrong trades.

1.3.1 What should you do?

The best way to avoid a regretful trading psychology is to accept that you can't have all the opportunities in the market. The equation in the stock markets is very simple – You win some; you lose some. Once you accept this rule, your trading psychology will automatically change for the better.

1.4 Hope

Investors often think that trading is gambling. It's because they hope to win all the time and when they don't, they get dejected.

1.4.1 What should you do?

To become a successful trader, you must have a solid trading psychology which is not dependent on hope. If you keep hoping for things to change in the near future, you're putting your entire investment at risk. Don't let hope keep you invested in a loss making trade. Be practical, and book your losses at the correct time. To attain and maintain success as a trader, you have to work hard to cultivate a mindset! Let's see how trading psychology helps you cultivate a better mindset!

2. How to Improve Your Trading Psychology

2.1 Get Yourself in the Right Mindset

Before you even start your trading day, simply remind yourself that markets are never constant. You will have some good days and some bad days, but the bad days too shall pass. Another effective strategy to improve your trading psychology is to give yourself time. You are not going to make a fortune on your very first trading day. You need to spend time and efforts in creating a rock solid trading strategy which isn't affected by the market sentiments. While you cannot completely eliminate emotions from trading, the goal is to reduce the extent of emotions controlling your trading psychology.

2.2 Have a Great knowledge Base

One of the best ways to improve your trading psychology is to increase your knowledge and trading skills. Having a strong knowledge base of the stock market is key to defeating negative trading psychology. Remember, knowledge is power!

2.3 Remind yourself that you are Trading in Real Money

When you're trading online, it's easy to forget that the numbers on your screen actually represent real money. There's nothing wrong in risking your money in hopes of generating returns. But remember to be cautious and make smarter investment decisions.

2.4 Observe the Habits of Successful Traders

Stock market is unique because it treats each trader differently. When it comes to trading, you should be aware of what your peers are doing, not to copy them but to learn from them. By observing the positive characteristics of successful traders and inculcating few habits or strategies into your own trading, you can improve your trading strategies manyfolds.

2.5 Practice! Practice! Practice!

Last but not the least, practice is the best and most reliable way to gain mental strength. It helps you improve your trading psychology over time as you build well practised trading strategies and are well prepared for any ups or downs.

Final Thoughts

Understanding trading psychology and implementing it is a time consuming process. You have to continuously refine your trading psychology over long time periods.

To sum up, remember these three golden principles of trading psychology

<u>Be disciplined</u>

<u>Be flexible</u>

<u>Never stop learning</u>

Best Wishes To All New Traders

www.ingramcontent.com/pod-product-compliance
Lightning Source LLC
Chambersburg PA
CBHW040739120726
48007CB00008B/138